READING TERMINAL AND MARKET

Philadelphia's Historic Gateway and Grand Convention Center

CAROL M. HIGHSMITH AND JAMES L. HOLTON

CHELSEA PUBLISHING, INC., WASHINGTON, D.C.

Reading Terminal and Market: Philadelphia's Historic Gateway and Grand Convention Center

Chelsea Publishing, Inc.
3299 K Street, NW
Washington, DC 20007

Design and composition: Meadows & Wiser, Washington, D.C.
Printer and binder: Lebanon Valley Offset

ISBN: 0–9620877–1–8

PENNSYLVANIA
CONVENTION
CENTER

Carol M. Highsmith, Project Director, is a Washington, D.C., architectural photographer whose lens has documented several monumental renovation projects, including the restoration of Pennsylvania Avenue. She and her husband, Ted Landphair, have co-authored four books: *Pennsylvania Avenue: America's Main Street, Union Station: A Decorative History of Washington's Grand Terminal, Embassies of Washington,* and a book that took them to every state in the United States, *America Restored,* all featuring Highsmith photographs. Their most recent work is a study of the Library of Congress.

James L. Holton is a veteran of more than 50 years in the news business, having worked as a writer on the *Reading Times* and the *Reading Eagle* in Reading, Pa.; editor for The Associated Press in Pittsburgh, and writer, editor, producer, and vice president during a 30-year career in radio and television with NBC News in New York and Washington. The author of *The Reading Railroad: History of a Coal Age Empire,* Holton is now retired in Reinholds, Pa., and paints scenes of Reading steam days while not engaged in various writing projects.

Cover. A local train from New Hope, Pa., led by a venerable Reading camelback (center cab) Engine 590, has just arrived in the terminal some time in the 1940s, as a newer electric-powered multiple-unit train across the platform prepares to depart. (Oil painting by Ted Xaras; Frank Weer Collection)

Endleaf. Virtually every one of the terminal's 13 tracks is occupied by a variety of passenger cars in this photograph taken a few years after the train shed was completed. It is probably a Friday afternoon, and the weekend excursions to resorts in the Poconos and South Mountain are being readied for departure. (Frank Weer Collection)

Frontice. The handsome Italianate face of the Reading head house, shown before "modernization" in the late 1940s, lent a sedate and comely aura to what had been an undistinguished neighborhood of shops and saloons along Market Street east of Philadelphia's City Hall. (Frank Weer Collection)

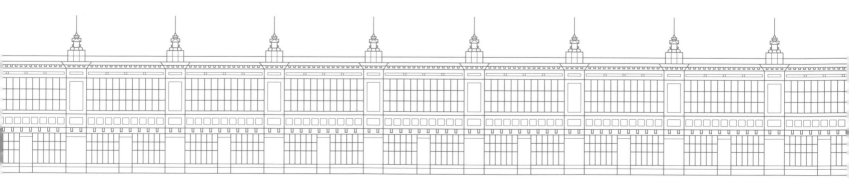

CONTENTS

ACKNOWLEDGMENTS

The authors are indebted to many people and organizations whose association with the terminal made them invaluable sources of information and lore in the writing and image-gathering for this book. Foremost among the organizations are the Hagley Museum and Library, Wilmington, Del.; the Reading Company Technical & Historical Society, Reading, Pa.; the Railroad Museum of Pennsylvania, Strasburg, Pa.; and the Reading Company, Philadelphia, among them custodians of most of the pertinent Reading archives. The Reading Terminal Market Merchants' Association, and the public-relations departments of SEPTA, Amtrak and Conrail also provided helpful information and advice.

Other Philadelphia institutions, including the Free Library of Philadelphia, the Atwater Kent Museum, the Pennsylvania Historical Society, The Library Company of Philadelphia, and the Urban Archives of the Temple University Library provided access to important vintage photographs and artifacts. Scores of individuals, many of them former Reading Railroad employees, contributed wonderful personal accounts of activity in the train shed in its glory days. The authors are especially thankful to Frank Weer and Robert J. Linden, whose expansive collections of Reading photographs and ephemera provided a pictorial dimension to their store of verbal nostalgia. Ted Xaras's photo collection and artwork were another treasure trove of pictorial memorabilia. David O'Neil, John E. "Jacko" Thompson, Ken Murry, John D. Denney, Jr., Jane Margaretten, Richard Short, Bruce G. Saylor, and Howard Pincus provided images that helped bring this book alive.

Jim Wunderle and Doug Humes of the Reading Company were important sources of information, along with other former Reading officials—such as Bill Dimeling and Bill Hankowski—from the post-bankruptcy years. People associated with the Reading Terminal Market who generously assisted included Bill Gardner of the market's management staff and Duane Perry and Harry Ochs of the Merchants' Association, Anne Bassett, Mike Strange and Noelle Margerum, standholders.

Many hours were spent behind the scenes photographing the process of construction and reconstruction. We thank Ceasar Maddox for cheerfully lugging heavy photography equipment around the unheated shed, and Dorothy Jones and David Hofeling, who worked with Carol Highsmith on all facets of publishing and photography. Deep appreciation also goes to Joyce and Bob Mozenter for opening their Chestnut Hill home to Highsmith during this complex undertaking.

Many individuals associated with the Convention Center Project were enormously helpful as well. Notable were Ted Garrison, who managed the construction, and Harry Perks and Bob Williams, who eased the authors' tasks along the way. The insights of master historic architect Hyman Myers were much appreciated.

We loved every second of the fascinating—and nostalgic—Reading Terminal and Market project and share Pennsylvanians' admiration of the spectacular finished product.

Workers appear like ghosts as they remove windows along the 12th Street side of the train shed prior to a meticulous restoration of the ornamental cast-iron sides of the building. (Carol M. Highsmith, Photographer)

THE PHILADELPHIA

AND

READING

RAIL ROAD.

Will be opened for Travel and the general Transportation of Freight,

On MONDAY, December 9, 1839.

WINTER ARRANGEMENT.

HOURS OF STARTING:

From Philadelphia at 6 A. M.

From Reading at . . . . 1½ P. M.

Depot in Philadelphia, corner of Broad & Cherry Sts.

FARES BETWEEN THE FOLLOWING PLACES:

	1st Class Cars.	2d Class Cars.			1st Class Cars.	2d Class Cars.
Reading & Philadelphia . .	$2 50	$2 00	Douglassville & Philad'a . .		$2 00	$1 50
" Norristown . . .	1 87½	1 50	Pottstown "	. . . .	1 75	1 37½
" Phœnixville . .	1 25	1 00	Phœnixville "	. . . .	1 25	1 00
" Pottstown	0 75	0 62½	Norristown "	. . . .	0 62½	0 50
" Douglassville . .	0 62½	0 50				

The SIX o'clock Train from Philadelphia, will stop for BREAKFAST at Norristown.

The 6 and 1½ o'clock Trains will stop at convenient points for Way Passengers;
also at Douglassville, Pottstown, Phœnixville, and opposite Norristown and Manayunk.

p

Passengers are requested to procure their TICKETS before the Trains start.

Young, Printer, Black Horse Alley, Philadelphia.

INTRODUCTION

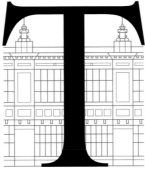

The old 3rd & Berks streets station of the North Pennsylvania Railroad, which the Reading used for its Bethlehem Branch and Jersey City service until construction of the Reading Terminal unified Philadelphia passenger facilities at 12th and Market. (Ted Xaras Collection)

T he United States in the years just before the birth of the 20th century was abubble with pride and confidence in itself. Seemingly overnight, the nation's mastery of the Industrial Revolution had made it a world economic and military leader. Its mills and factories were producing goods at a pace and quality that had become the envy of the globe.

Lacing together this burgeoning industrial empire was a rapidly expanding system of railroads, with most of the big trunk lines engaged in a fierce competition for power and wealth.

One manifestation of this corporate rivalry was architectural braggadocio, a phenomenon in which giant railroads were building magnificent palaces for their passenger trains, their riders, and, most of all, their own corporate images. To railroad tycoons, those grandiose depots were intended to be the symbols of a new kind of business institution whose lofty mission placed them above the level of common manufactures and vendors of ordinary wares.

In the 1880s and nineties, great terminals were built in many of the nation's large cities, most impressively the huge Union Station in Saint Louis, North and South stations in Boston, Chicago's Grand Central, and the Pennsylvania's handsome Broad Street Station at its headquarters in Philadelphia.

And then in the early 1890s, just three blocks from the Pennsy's imposing edifice, a new train shed, promising to be the biggest of them all and fronted by a splendid pink and white, eight-story company office building—the "head house"—boldly entered the competition. The terminal complex would be built by a small regional railroad that seemed altogether unsuited to be a player in such a high-stakes game.

The company was the Philadelphia & Reading—commonly known as just the Reading—a pioneer railway in eastern Pennsylvania and New Jersey that had prospered early in the Industrial Revolution by dint of its domination of the vital anthracite coal trade, but which had fallen on hard times in the 1880s.

There seemed to be little justification for this impoverished carrier to gamble its modest finances on what would be an imposing and expensive showcase to an uncertain future. The revelation of the company's real rationale for the elaborate downtown depot—an ambitious expansion scheme that came to light while it was abuilding—would be only the first in a series of surprising and sometimes dramatic adventures that would swirl around the Reading Terminal during the hundred years it would be a dominant physical presence on East Market Street.

An estimated eight million people would enter or leave through the terminal's massive oak doors in its 91 years of life. Those who rode Reading passenger cars would figure in countless human dramas that were played out on the train platforms and in the passenger lobby, especially during the five wartime periods when men and women in uniform swelled ridership. Housewives by the thousands shopped each week in the unique basement of the train shed, where the internationally renowned Reading Terminal Market enabled them not only to fill their market baskets with choice viands, but also to send the food home on Reading suburban trains for free.

In the terminal's final years as a commuter station in the 1960s and seventies, it could not remain altogether aloof from the changes in the neighborhood on the Reading's side of City Hall—a physical deterioration that accompanied a general decline in Center City business. In just a few years the great Reading Terminal went from being the Grande Dame of Market Street to a bag lady on Arch Street, struggling to survive.

But unlike most of the other grand turn-of-the-century depots, the Reading Terminal with its historic train shed continued to stand long after it ceased to serve railroad patrons, with the venerable Reading Terminal Market still operating underneath the abandoned tracks. And now the historic terminal, with a revitalized market functioning more briskly than ever, has taken on a lively new role befitting her one-time status.

The transformation has been as much a result of the evolution of urban realities—plus considerable good luck—as it is a testament to the wisdom and vision of the railroaders who built the terminal. Indeed, its metamorphosis into the grand entranceway for the exuberant new Pennsylvania Convention Center, after years of neglect and threats of imminent destruction, seems almost miraculous.

In words and photographs, this book memorializes the great depot's long history as a transportation hub and its dazzling conversion into the very symbol of a new Philadelphia.

It is somehow fitting that the imposing Reading Terminal train shed, which served as a comfortable vestibule to the world for a half-dozen generations of 20th-century Pennsylvanians, will become the gateway to a different kind of 21st-century world exhibited in the Pennsylvania Convention Center.

here is nothing in corporate records to reveal exactly when or how it came about, but some time in 1887 a new management team for the Philadelphia & Reading Railroad decided to build in its home base of Philadelphia "the finest railway structure in America, if not the world." The company's announcement promised that the new station would be a magnificent edifice, in the grand style of the great trunk lines of the day.

When word of the plan had first leaked from the company's rundown, cramped headquarters building on South Fourth Street, the railroad world was astonished and dubious. Everybody in the business community knew the formerly prosperous coal road was still trying to shake off the effects of its second bankruptcy in less than a decade, and was desperately in need of outside financial help just to keep its trains running. How could the company justify such an extravagant undertaking?

There was one rationale that would have satisfied some reasonable critics: the need to consolidate the road's Philadelphia passenger facilities, which were woefully inadequate for handling the Reading's growing share of the commuter-rail business. Most of the railroad's branch lines fanned out to the northwest and northeast of the city, but they terminated downtown at three widely separated depots—Broad and Callowhill streets, Ninth and Green streets, and Third and Berks streets. All had grown old and inefficient.

Above. Austin Corbin, installed as Reading president in 1887, initiated a plan for a modest consolidated passenger depot in downtown Philadelphia. (Hagley Museum and Library)

Opposite. Scene along Market Street during excavation of the old 12th Street Market. It would become the site of the great Reading head house. There is little evidence seen of mechanized resources to supplement manual labor. (Frank Weer Collection)

Overleaf. Reading Terminal builder Charles McCaul prepared a lithograph of his new masterpiece, which companies like glass and lamp importer R. L. Allen, Son & Co. distributed to their clients, complete with now-faded notations of the building's many glories. (John E. "Jacko" Thompson Collection)

The Reading's worry about its own passenger problems was exacerbated by the sudden growth of commuter business on the Pennsylvania Railroad, the Reading's traditional rival for the Philadelphia trade. The competition had intensified after the Pennsylvania began constructing its impressive Broad Street Station facing City Hall in 1881, rapidly expanding the Pennsy's daily commuter service to businessmen who had begun to move from the city to small towns on its westward Main Line.

Before the Pennsylvania became a national trunk line by expanding across Pennsylvania and into the Midwest in the middle of the 19th century, it and the Reading had been relatively equal in wealth, operational proficiency, and reputation. The Pennsy's new Broad Street terminal was impressive by Philadelphia standards, but it was hardly exemplary for the "Standard Railroad of the World." Its train shed contained nine tracks, covered by a double-canopied roof, with a four-story head house festooned with Victorian turrets. And when the Reading formed the Philadelphia & Reading Terminal Railroad Company as the corporate vehicle for its projected Market Street station, Pennsylvania Railroad President George Roberts ordered his construction people to begin drafting plans for an even grander Broad Street Station that would be, if nothing else, bigger than the new Reading depot.

Thus, streamlining the Reading's own commuter service by consolidating its city depots at a single location made good competitive sense, even in the face of the company's straitened financial condition. But was the project just a case of corporate one-upmanship—designed to be bigger and more elegant than Broad Street Station—or was something else afoot?

It turns out there was: a bold scheme that before long would startle the railroad industry—with disastrous results for the Reading—and even shake the financial stability of the entire country.

J. Pierpont Morgan, the legendary New York financier and railroad titan, was personally orchestrating the Reading reorganization. In 1886 he persuaded Austin Corbin, a 60-year-old, New Hampshire-born lawyer-turned-banker who had become involved in railroading, to accept the presidency of the Reading road. At the time Corbin was also involved in building commuter towns on Long Island, and conveniently was president of the Long Island Railroad. So he tried to manage the Reading from his Long Island Railroad office on Wall Street.

Corbin prudently installed as his chief deputy and surrogate at Philadelphia an unknown but highly competent hands-on railroader. He was a handsome and personable young Canadian named Archibald Angus McLeod, who had worked in various blue-collar jobs on several Midwest-U.S. railroads before catching Corbin's eye.

This odd, long-distance management team had taken over after the disastrous 1870s, when the Reading had expanded recklessly into the business of mining anthracite (hard) coal, then an important industrial fuel and the principal means of home heating in the Northeast. The gambit so weakened its cash flow that the company fell into receivership twice in four years.

The Reading proposal called for construction of two elevated rail lines along a Y-shaped viaduct, meeting at 12th and Callowhill and extending southward to 12th and Market Streets, where the new terminal would be built. But political problems quickly arose when the Philadelphia City Council, which had to approve the whole terminal project, voiced a variety of objections: concern about the dangers of additional downtown grade crossings; about the eviction of merchants and householders along Ninth Street to make way for the project; and, finally, about the wisdom of destroying the city's two most popular markets, both of which were located at the projected depot site at 12th and Market.

There was much insinuation by friends of the Reading that George Roberts and Company over at Pennsy were responsible for many of these roadblocks. Whether out of frustration or not, in the spring of 1890 Corbin resigned his Reading post, and Archie McLeod, the former track laborer, was elected to replace him.

McLeod wrote an impassioned letter to the Common Council—the more powerful body of what was then an unusual bicameral council in Philadelphia—pointing out the benefits—including elimination of several grade crossings—that the public would enjoy as a result of construction of the terminal and viaduct. Three weeks after McLeod sent his letter, the ordinance passed, thus breaking a three-year blockade of the Reading Terminal project.

McLeod then turned his attention to the negotiations with the two markets' owners and concessionaires. In March 1891, he proposed a unique solution: $1 million in reparations, and construction of a single new market on the ground level of the terminal, below the big train shed. The lawsuit was dropped, and one of Reading depot's most famous and cherished features—the world-famous Reading Terminal Market—was born.

Early in 1891, contracts were let for the heavy work—construction of the roadway, head house and train shed; and for structural and decorative ironwork. A contract with Wilson Brothers & Company, civil engineers and architects, for overall design, had been formalized months before, as had been the engagement of chief architect F. H. Kimball.

Even as the Reading Terminal began to take form, Archibald McLeod turned to the most crucial task of all: financing. Ignoring Morgan—about whom he huffed, "I would rather run a peanut stand than be dictated to by J. P. Morgan"—McLeod persuaded Provident Life and Trust Company—with participation from Drexel & Company—to issue $8.5 million in bonds to the terminal company.

Soon some of the Reading's reasons for undertaking so grandiose a project became clearer, for, beginning in 1890, McLeod had begun a spectacular acquisition campaign intended to transform the old coal road into a regional trunk line.

In just a few months, McLeod had grabbed control of the New Jersey Central and Lehigh Valley railroads, and the Reading had grown from a modest carrier with fewer than a thousand miles of track to a vast system covering 2,485 miles. It now controlled about 75 percent of the nation's vital coal business, as well as a large part of the important Hudson River shorefront at Jersey City. By early 1892, the Philadelphia & Reading Railroad employed an army of more than 100,000 workers—the largest work force under one management in the world.

McLeod's seemingly reckless scheme for an imposing new head house and train shed on Market Street began to make more sense. And, by gaining control of the Boston & Maine Railroad and several smaller neighboring roads, he soon revealed that his ultimate sights were set as far afield as the heart of New England.

These stunning moves, of course, opened exciting vistas for long-distance passenger trains operating out of the new Reading Terminal on Market Street.

There, beneath the skeleton of the train shed early in 1892, a makeshift food market, from which the elaborate Reading Terminal Market would grow, took root.

An interesting note in President McLeod's correspondence files from Chief Engineer John Wilson reveals how individual tastes entered into decisions about the overall project: "[Architect] Kimball has recommended white terra cotta and pink brick [above the third floor of the head house]. I have not seen it used myself, but I am disposed to defer to Mr. Kimball's judgment and taste . . . and consider it desirable to get away from the buff, which is getting to be very common."

McLeod got special satisfaction in knowing that, for the time being, he had a bigger and more handsome terminal than George Roberts, his old nemesis at the Pennsylvania. The latter's construction crews three blocks westward were feverishly at work on a massive canopy that eventually would surpass the Reading Terminal's 256-foot roof, but the Reading would win the race to finish first. Its new train shed was hailed by local newspapers as the largest single-span structure of its type in the world, and its stately head house "one of the handsomest terminal passenger stations" anywhere on the globe.

By the end of '92, the train shed was nearing completion and crews were working to finish the head house. But Archie McLeod had more than a new terminal to worry about. He was confronting a campaign engineered by Pierpont Morgan to derail his expansion project and was desperately trying to find new funding sources as the Reading's bankers tightened their noose.

Preoccupation with this crisis may explain why he missed the momentous events of January 27, 1893. At 3:45 that Friday afternoon, a light passenger engine with the Pullman car *Mildred* in tow stopped at the throat of the terminal above Arch Street while mid-level city and company dignitaries stepped aboard. Archibald McLeod was nowhere to be seen. The one-car special eased out on the elevated approach track and made a brief tour of the three-pronged trackage that would soon bring the first passengers into the train shed.

The official inauguration of regular Reading Terminal train service took place two days later, with most of the normal Sunday Main Line trains operating in and out of the depot for the first time. A group of chilled but excited train-watchers huddled to keep warm on Platform 1 awaiting the pre-dawn departure of the first train. Precisely at 4 a.m., engineer Michael Welsh pulled No. 139, the Harrisburg and Shamokin Express, out of the train shed. Behind No. 139's four day coaches rode the private car *Bonvenue,* assigned to General Superintendent M. F. Bonzano. He and a few other middle managers made up the only Reading Company contingent recognizing the moment.

McLeod was again conspicuously absent, and the *Philadelphia Public Ledger* noted in its account: "There was great surprise manifested that there was no ceremony of any kind arranged by the company to mark the importance of the event, but it was explained that the incomplete state of the depot rendered it impossible to signalize the event in a manner commensurate with its importance."

There was no mention that the top officials of the company, especially its president, were busy elsewhere even at that early hour of a Sunday morning, desperately fighting for their corporate lives.

The first engine to enter the Reading train shed was No. 159, which pulled a work train into place on temporary rails located about where Track No.1 would eventually be constructed. (Reading Company Technical & Historical Society Collection)

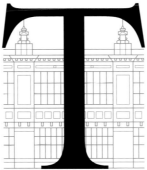

housands of curious Philadelphians poured into the Reading Terminal waiting room and onto the train platform on that Sunday, January 30, 1893, just to gawk at the action and marvel at the splendor of it all. But all was not well behind the scenes. Three weeks later, on February 20 following pressure from J. P. Morgan, the banking firms that had advanced money for the Reading's New England adventure refused President McLeod's pleas for more time to pay the railroad's monthly obligation, and the old coal road was plunged into receivership for the third time in 13 years.

News of the Reading's failure stunned Wall Street and is blamed by business historians for triggering the nationwide "Panic of '93," one of the longest and deepest depressions in the country's history.

It was ironic that, by the time the plush president's office on the fourth floor had been ready for occupancy that summer, the man who had battled to erect the great depot—and who had personally designed the office's rococo decor and curved exterior—was in no position to enjoy its appointments. McLeod, who was forced to resign in August, left Philadelphia for a life of quiet retirement in New York.

Most of the vestiges of his empire disappeared quickly. The courts voided the takeovers in New Jersey and New England, as well as the Reading's control of the Lehigh Valley road, and the Reading shrank back to its pre-expansion size. Its third receivership lasted three years until, in 1896, a new holding company was created—by the same J. P. Morgan who had pressured the railroad into bankruptcy—to look after the Reading and its coal-and-iron subsidiary.

There is little activity—and not a single motorized vehicle—seen in this early three-quarters view of the head house and the west wall of the market and train shed visible along 12th Street in the background. The ornately rounded alcove that sits imperiously in the corner, offset at the fourth-floor level, was the president's office. (Historical Society of Pennsylvania)

Opposite. *The numerous American flags and generally empty sidewalks suggest that this turn-of-the-century photograph was taken on a summer holiday. One curiosity is the apparent similarity in the designs of the awnings on a few of the head house's office windows and on the Vendig Hotel, a haven for railroad travelers, on the west side of 12th Street. (Ted Xaras Collection)*

MARKET STREET FROM CITY HALL ARCH, PHILADELPHIA, PA.

2544

Above. *Vintage postcard shows a more distant view of the east side of Market Street, taken through the east portal of City Hall. (David O'Neil Collection)*

Remarkably, the handsome new Reading Terminal, including its market, escaped any direct financial blows from the bankruptcy. When the Philadelphia & Reading Terminal Railroad Company had been created five years earlier, it was organized and financed in a way that left it untouched by the foreclosure proceedings against the parent company.

The eight-story building fronting the Reading's train shed was an architectural departure from the Victorian turrets, spires, and gingerbread adornments that were customary in railway-terminal buildings around the turn of the century. A box-shaped structure replete with graceful arches and setbacks, including a long loggia at the second level overlooking Market Street, the head house was of the late-Italian Renaissance style. The building's face was trimmed with ornately carved terra cotta, and the whole edifice was topped with a handsome balustrade along all four façades.

Most striking of all was its rich pink-and-white exterior that loomed above Market Street's otherwise drab buildings. The first four stories were faced with pink granite, and the four upper floors with pink bricks. Trimming was cast into generous expanses of terra cotta. The building's first floor contained a wide formal entrance onto Market Street, opening into a passenger lobby, ticketing office, and baggage rooms. A cab stand and an inside carriageway—running the width of the building from 11th to 12th streets—were located on the north side.

The second floor housed two large waiting rooms (one just for "ladies"), reached by a wide stairway and an elevator. Operating quarters for the railroad and terminal companies were based on a mezzanine a half-story above the second floor, and the remainder of the building held express offices and other railroad-related businesses.

The first two floors of the head house were linked to the train shed by a 50-foot lobby running the width of the train platform; in it, passengers would wait to be admitted to trackside through intricate wrought-iron gates. Track 13 was reserved for U.S. Mail cars; the terminal's 12 other tracks were set in pairs, separated by asphalt platforms.

Part of the heavily reinforced train platform served as the ceiling of the terminal market below. Soaring the equivalent of nine stories above the tracks was the gracefully arched roof of the train shed. Daylight beamed onto the activities below through five rows of skylights. The 509-foot-long roof was supported by pairs of massive trusses set 50 feet apart, with the horizontal thrust at the foot of each arch taken up by a system of I-bar ties running beneath the train-shed floor.

The first regular train service at 12th and Market in late January had been little more than a token offering of a few trains to Philadelphia's exclusive Main Line suburbs. The full slate of upriver trains did not reach the terminal until a key connection to the Norristown line was constructed a few weeks later at Wallace Street, which then allowed service to the depot from the Norristown and Bethlehem branches, as well as from the important New York Division.

In May 1893 the train shed was brightened by the appearance of the handsome "Royal Blue" fleet of fast Washington-to-Jersey City trains developed by the Baltimore & Ohio Railroad. To get these expresses to the Reading Terminal meant changing their cars from the B&O's new 4−4−0 locomotives to ordinary Reading shifters that backed the Royal Blues into the big train shed. After taking on passengers, the beautifully appointed blue, gray, and gold cars would be headed by a Reading engine for the high-speed run to the Hudson shore. Unfortunately the time lost in these maneuvers only diminished the race with the Pennsylvania— which operated its own handsomely appointed expresses to Jersey City —and the splendid Royal Blue livery disappeared from the Reading Terminal by 1895.

But other glamorous long-distance trains, including the "New England Daily Express" and long-distance Pullman connections to the Great Lakes via the New York Central and Lehigh Valley lines, remained part of the Reading's passenger-train schedules for many years. In fact, sleepers on the "Maple Leaf" to Toronto and Chicago, and parlor cars on the "Black Diamond" to Buffalo and Niagara Falls, continued to leave the terminal daily until the Lehigh Valley ended long-distance passenger service in 1961.

By the early years of the new century, the Reading was running daylong "clocker" service to and from Jersey City—one train each hour, on the hour, between 7 a.m. and 7 p.m., each equipped with Pullman parlor cars offering various levels of meal service.

In addition to the train shed and its operations, other facets of the terminal in the 1920s fast won devoted followings. There was the market, of course, with its throng of loyal housewives and servants dependent upon its fresh groceries, meats, and other fine foods. Acclaimed, too, were the epicurean offerings dispensed in George Knoblauch's gracious, unnamed white-tablecloth restaurant adjacent to the waiting room. This fine dining room would last in considerable gustatory glory for 41 years.

Passenger business improved after the terminal began handling the bulk of the Reading's Philadelphia traffic, but there were plenty of growing pains that persisted well into the 1900s. One turn-of-the-century problem, prompted by the need for untrained labor coupled with political unrest in Europe, was the frequent arrival of impoverished immigrants in organized groups, bound for upstate jobs. Their appearance in the sedate precincts of the terminal's waiting room visibly upset some passengers awaiting trains to the tonier suburbs in Bucks County, or the spotless row homes of Pennsylvania Dutch country upriver. A letter from a minor station official to First Vice President Theodore Voorhees bluntly expressed a commonly held view:

They are filthy and unfit to occupy seats which are supposed to be used by other passengers. Last Sunday there was quite a number of these emigrants with their children, some of them were so filthy one could see the lice crawling on their clothes.

The stationmaster found a separate waiting room for the immigrants, and the problem was never again mentioned.

There were early, serious physical problems with the train shed. Only two years after its completion, the canopy's iron trusses began to rust due to a chemical reaction to the gases in the locomotives' exhaust smoke. The entire train shed was repainted in the summer of 1895, only to have the problem reappear that fall. This sparked a flurry of memos, meetings, and consultations with experts until it was decided that two additional coats of paint—to include red lead, lamp black, and linseed oil—would be necessary.

31

The roof—especially its tin-sheeting cover—also had begun to deteriorate. Tin reacted badly to the toxic gases, and terminal engineers, after consulting with their peers at the Broad Street Station—which had confronted the same difficulties—replaced the tin with slag and added wired glass to the skylights. Ventilators wcre redesigned to allow more air into areas of the roof where locomotive exhaust was heaviest, and the deterioration problem was eased.

Similar problems cropped up underfoot in 1902. Vendors in the market below the train floor had been complaining of leaks dripping onto their foodstuffs, sometimes in veritable torrents. The first remedy was a new ornamental-tin ceiling. That proved inadequate, and it was finally decided that the drainage problem would have to be dealt with directly. The solution meant re-laying the entire 6,000 feet of track, plus the asphalt platforms and the concrete beds on which the tracks were set. Afterward, while some leaking was still reported from time to time, the difficulty was deemed mostly resolved.

The Reading Terminal's masters continually sought improvements, provided they did not cost too much. Some came about in unusual fashion.

An example was the installation in 1897 of a handsome Seth Thomas street clock on the Market Street sidewalk near the corner of 12th Street. It would become, along with the market and the great train shed, one of the familiar landmarks of Center City Philadelphia. How the clock got there is not widely known. It was prompted by an editorial in the *Philadelphia Evening Bulletin* of March 27th, possibly written by a newspaperman who had missed his homebound train. It read:

WANTED — A TERMINAL CLOCK

It would be a great convenience to thousands of persons daily hurrying to and from the Reading Terminal Station if the front of that splendid building contained a clock as visible as the dials of the clock in the tower of the Broad Street station.

Exactly why so obviously needed a convenience for the public was not provided for in the equipment of the well-appointed station is not clear. Certainly the absence of it is a daily cause of complaint, especially as there is now no clock of large size and accurate movement anywhere in the vicinity.

This public embarrassment—especially the unfavorable comparison to the Pennsy station's tower clock—brought rapid reaction. First thing Monday morning, Voorhees asked Superintendent E. F. Smith if a clock ever had been contemplated, with an obvious hint that perhaps it should be.

It just happened that such a clock, standing outside the Broad Street ticket office jointly operated by the Reading and the B&O, was about to be disposed of because of an impending move of the office to another location. The Reading bought the B&O's half ownership in the oversized timepiece, and it soon was moved to 12th and Market outside the new terminal.

The four-track approach viaduct with its dog-leg at the open end of the train shed is shown in this photograph taken shortly after the turn of the century. Locomotives are drifting down to the terminal, and coaches on the approach tracks are being readied for train assignments just before the start of the afternoon commuter rush. (James L. Holton Collection)

Right. Night view from a colorized postcard shows Market Street looking west toward City Hall, with the busy Reading Terminal on the right, midway down the block. (David O'Neil Collection)

It was in 1897, too, that bookkeepers tallied up the tab for the entire terminal project. The figure: $7,676,584.79. That included the cost of building the train shed and market house, the head house, the viaduct, and spur lines running into the terminal, cold-storage facilities for the terminal market—as well as real estate, administrative, and legal costs.

The train lobby in those years underwent continuous change as the perceived needs of passengers evolved. In the years leading up to World War I, little else changed in the terminal and its services to Reading Company passengers, except for the addition of dining-car service on several routes, and marked improvement in the motive power and rolling equipment that appeared in the train shed. In the interest of safety, passenger cars became much heavier as steel construction largely replaced wood. This, in turn, required bigger and more powerful locomotives of the Pacific 4–6–2 type, capable of handling heavier trains at higher speeds.

The Great War itself had little visible effect on depot operations beyond the dramatic increase in the number of men in uniform among the passengers—and the technical fact that the U.S. Government ran the railroads. But because it was a "stub-end" station, Reading Terminal saw few troop trains hauling military units on wartime maneuvers. It did, however, lose many of its employees to service in the war.

The 1920s saw the high point of passenger patronage on the Reading, as well as on other American railroads. This was before Americans' widespread use of the automobile for personal travel, or the popularity of cheap and reliable air travel. The Reading Terminal handled about 300 inbound and outbound trains every weekday throughout the decade.

Then there was the "Seven O'Klockers' Club." It was made up of a group of 100 regular commuters between Philadelphia and Jersey City—connecting from there to New York City. In 1920 they arranged for their exclusive use an observation-club car on the 7:00 a.m. eastbound train out of the terminal, and on the 6:12 return trip out of Jersey City in the evening. They elected officers, held their own holiday parties, and provided breakfast to members on the morning trip and suitable libations along with card games on the way home in the evening. After the first year it was calculated that the club would post a collective total of almost five million miles a year aboard their splendidly appointed private car. The Seven O'Klockers—who were mostly stockbrokers, bankers, investment analysts, and other businessmen working on or near Wall Street—would continue their fraternal commutes on the Reading for another 45 years.

After 1916, most of the "Yorkers" (cars on New York Division runs) were hauled by the new, Pacific-class engines. But those magnificent machines would soon share their terminal berths with units powered by a new kind of transportation technology: electrical propulsion.

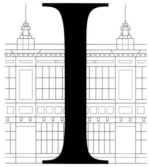

Ifthere is any one thing that sets Reading Terminal apart from other great railroad depots, it would have to be the gastronomic bazaar tucked away in its cellar. Today the Reading Terminal Market is one of the most endearing institutional treasures in Philadelphia, but that was not always so.

In fact, in 1892 when the deal was completed to provide a new home under the train shed for the two old markets that had previously squatted on the 12th-and-Market site, the railroad company opened its new "hall of victualers" before the structure even had permanent walls or a roof overhead.

The market's story goes back to the founding of the city itself. When William Penn's managers established the town of Philadelphia in the late 1600s, one of their first actions was to herd the ragtag crowd of farmers, fishermen and huntsmen—who were hawking their goods all over the bustling settlement—into an open area at the foot of what was known as High Street, hard by the Delaware River. Soon the so-called "Jersey Market" (most of the hucksters were from that neighboring state) acquired a roof and began to expand westward in the middle of the thoroughfare that had been appropriately renamed Market Street.

By the middle of the 19th century the string of market sheds had become six blocks long, making the easternmost mile of the city's main street a veritable babble of farmers and food purveyors on most days. Bowing to complaints of nearby residents, city fathers decreed that the street markets would have to go, and summarily dismantled them.

Lena Zook, a young Amish woman from Lancaster County, toils at a stand featuring fresh-baked soft pretzels, a Philadelphia delicacy. She is brushing butter on the still-warm pretzels, which locals customarily eat slathered with generous daubs of mustard. (Carol M. Highsmith, Photographer)

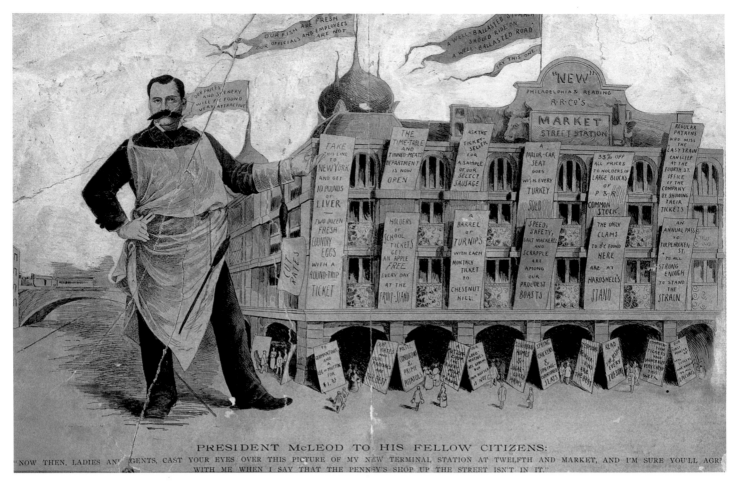

PRESIDENT McLEOD TO HIS FELLOW CITIZENS:

"NOW THEN, LADIES AND GENTS, CAST YOUR EYES OVER THIS PICTURE OF MY NEW TERMINAL STATION AT TWELFTH AND MARKET, AND I'M SURE YOU'LL AGREE WITH ME WHEN I SAY THAT THE PENN'Y'S SHOP UP THE STREET ISN'T IN IT."

A number of marketplace buildings soon sprang up in Center City. The most prominent and modern was the Farmers' Market, which put up a handsome brick building in 1860 on the north side of Market Street, east of 12th. Another, called the Franklin Market, soon erected a mart along 12th Street, fronting on Market alongside the Farmers' Market, and running north to Filbert Street. It claimed to be the biggest markethouse in the world. Both places flourished in their noisy and aromatic proximity to one another.

Then along came the railroad and its plan to build a huge new depot on the block where the two markets stood. The companies that owned the markets held out for a price of more than $2 million for the properties. Reading President McLeod offered a compromise—$1 million plus erection by the railroad of a new combined markethouse under the train shed, to be operated as a full-fledged part of the Philadelphia & Reading conglomerate. Everybody agreed, and work began almost immediately.

Even as demolition of the old market stalls between Market and Filbert streets started in August of that year, construction began on a temporary location for the food vendors on the terminal site north of Filbert.

When the Philadelphia & Reading revealed its intention to build its new downtown depot atop a market, the rival Pennsylvania Railroad responded with political roadblocks as well as public ridicule, a sample of which is shown here. The newspaper cartoon features a caricature of the Reading's doughty president, A. A. McLeod. (Ken Murry Collection)

On a cold and rainy George Washington's Birthday, February 22, 1892, the new market building was opened for business, with 795 stands marked off in 78,000 square feet of space. Some of the prospective new tenants were lineal descendants of marketers whose trade had begun on the banks of the Delaware two centuries earlier.

But all was not well with the new venture because of the haste with which it was started. In a kind of reverse domino effect, the market part of the project had been pushed along precipitously in order to clear the Market Street end of the site to make way for the foundations for the head house, where the old markets had been located.

As a consequence, the new cold-storage plant, which would be vital to the success of the market, had not been installed. And with the train shed not yet roofed at that early stage of construction, and only temporary walls to protect the perimeters of the market, there was little effective shelter against the elements. Although 490 vendors had signed up for space in the market, only a small contingent made the move on opening day.

But things became more rational shortly afterward when the market acquired its first full-time superintendent, George H. McKay, who had held a similar job at the highly regarded Washington Market in the nation's capital. McKay, who would hold his new Philadelphia job for 30 years, knew his business, and he was not a man to be pushed around. He was able to convince company officials that running a good market was just as important as running a good railroad; and he was instrumental in the establishment of formal company policy assuring that the market "maintain the highest standards in quality and merchandising."

As McKay saw to it that the kinks were worked out in the construction schedule—especially once the huge new cold-storage plant was installed and operating—the prospective new tenants began flocking eagerly to their assigned stalls. That refrigeration facility was by far the biggest in Philadelphia, with its half-million cubic feet of space and 52 separate rooms, each cooled to individual temperatures (15–25° for meat and poultry, 34° for fruits and vegetables). The refrigeration system included an array of special pumps, compressors and other equipment to handle the brine and ammonia used in its operation. Electricity for the machinery was supplied by the terminal's power plant and generators at Cherry Street.

When the cold-storage facility reached full stride a few years later, a visitor to its chilly climes would regularly find stored there 200,000 pounds of meat, 50,000 crates of eggs, thousands of cans of cream, 10,000 to 20,000 boxes of poultry; 10,000 barrels of berries and cherries; 25,000 barrels of apples and 20,000 tons of ice.

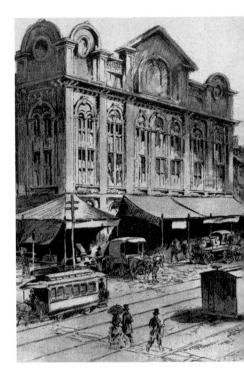

The Farmers' Market House, one of the two original markets displaced by the Reading Terminal and Market, is shown in a newspaper drawing from the 1880s. (Reading Railroad Employees' Magazine)

But despite good intentions on both sides, relations between the merchants and the Reading were marked by misunderstandings and occasional confrontations. Just three years after the market opened there were rumors about the possibility of widespread defections to a new market nearby. The superintendent acknowledged that there had been some dissatisfaction about rents. But he rationalized the company's position: "Our rents are considered high, but it is an expensive location, and taken altogether as a retail market, it is an expensive market. The established dealers do a large business, and can afford to pay high rents. We give them lower rates and much better service in the cold storage than they can obtain elsewhere in the city, and this they appreciate."

McKay took a more sympathetic tack a few days later in a memorandum to his boss, the railroad's first vice president:

Our market house is dark and dingy looking, on account of the worn out condition of the paint. When under construction in 1892 we were very much hurried. Exposed to the weather as the train shed was, without any roof for six or eight months, and with the side walls only temporarily covered, the painting could not be properly done.

I think as a matter of justice to our tenants, considering the high rents we are getting, that a portion of the market house should be painted this fall.

Train-floor attendants upstairs found another market-related annoyance to complain about early on. Confused people toting empty market baskets were found wandering about the depot waiting rooms, train concourse, and even the boarding platforms as they searched for the market. That prompted a rash of sign painting by the terminal staff intended to direct shoppers to their destination.

The railroad's tie to the market was always obvious to its customers, particularly from the rumbling and rattling in the ceiling as trains came and went on the train floor directly above. That sound became commonplace to habitués of the food hall, offering an almost comforting rhythm to the redolent life among the busy greengrocers and butchers and their patrons.

Business flourished as suburban housewives began to take advantage of another aspect of the railroad's involvement in the market—a free market-basket service on the suburban trains. Under that system, the homemaker could arrange for her grocery order to be filled in the market, and the basket placed aboard a train bound for her town and held at the station until she picked it up. In later years the company levied a small fee for carrying the basket. Under company rules, parcels would be held at the destination station for up to 30 days, which, if they contained once-fresh foodstuffs, was a pungently liberal policy indeed.

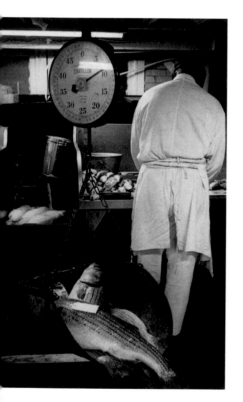

Fresh seafood has always been a staple for patrons of the terminal market, as may be seen in this photograph taken in the 1970s. (Jane Margaretten, Photographer)

Below. Shortages in World War II occasionally produced scenes such as this outside the market, when hard-to-get butter went on sale at one of the stands. (Urban Archives, Temple University, Philadelphia)

Left. William B. Margerum, "Victualer," serves two patrons at his stand around 1900. Margerum was one of the original standholders, and his descendants are among the market's merchants today. (Courtesy of Noelle Margerum)

Two restaurants and a sandwich counter were the only places to get a meal in the market in the early 1900s. The rest of the stalls along the 12 aisles were devoted to a wide variety of foodstuffs, from sausages sold by Chester County Amish farmers to fresh Delaware Bay oysters.

As horse-drawn wagons gave way to refrigerated trucks in the years after World War I, the market was able to improve its earlier unreliable attempts at a home delivery system within the city. The trucks provided service every hour to some 60 suburban towns and to resorts along the Jersey shore.

The Reading Company and the Reading Terminal Market Merchants' Association jointly celebrated the market's 40th anniversary in November 1931 with a week-long "Food and Home Progress Exposition," which drew tens of thousands of people from all over the region to the demonstrations and food displays in 1,000 booths. The Locomotive Shop Band came down from Reading to tootle enthusiastically, and a variety of prominent politicians and Philadelphia business leaders gave speeches.

A proud Reading president, Agnew T. Dice, bragged that the railroad's unique food emporium had won nationwide fame, noting that it was the biggest market in Pennsylvania, and the largest under one roof in the country. He said:

This week some of these merchants have been receiving green goods from Mexico. Here you will find deer meat from the Arctic, nuts from Africa, dairy products and delicacies from Europe, nuts and fruits from the Argentine and Brazil, while China, India, Arabia and I know not how many other countries send their best for the table to these counters.

What were the delicacies for the rich alone a few years ago have become staple winter foods for all.

The Depression years of the 1930s were difficult for the railroad and market alike, but both institutions managed to struggle through the hard times. By the end of that decade, in fact, 10 of the 64 merchants in the market were among the original standholders from 1892.

During World War II, the market became a mecca for Philadelphians seeking relief from the rigors of rationing. Even with the war on, the vendors at 12th and Market managed to provide a surprising variety of scarce victuals. Despite manpower shortages and other problems brought on by the war, 97 percent of the stalls were occupied even in 1944, the penultimate year of the conflict.

In the 1960s the Reading fell under the same economic pall that afflicted most of the other railroads of the Northeast, and the market got scant attention from the railroad. The great cold-storage facility at the market was shut down and dismantled; its space was subsequently used for dry storage and an electrical substation. Standholders then had to provide their own walk-in refrigeration facilities.

It is the Christmas rush in 1948, and holiday business was booming at the poultry-cutting stand operated by William G. Ziegler. Sanitation regulations then were far less stringent than they are today. (Urban Archives, Temple University, Philadelphia)

A severe cash shortage and declining freight and passenger traffic finally forced the railroad company into bankruptcy in 1971, after which the market suffered from almost total inattention from upstairs.

In 1976 the Reading ceased to exist as a railroad corporation. Its transportation assets were folded into the Consolidated Rail Corporation (Conrail). But a new Reading Company continued functioning, essentially as a real estate business, with Reading Terminal and Market as one of its prime assets.

Various ideas were floated by the bankrupt company to dispose of the market in one way or another, either as an outright sale, or by simply abolishing it altogether in order to make it easier to sell the terminal building. And as the months of uncertainty and neglect dragged on, business in what had become a shabby mercantile atmosphere rapidly dwindled.

For a few years in the late 1970s, the company leased the market to Samuel Rappaport, a Philadelphia real estate speculator, but the market declined even further. During those grim years, Rappaport at least got credit for having kept the market from total abandonment.

Finally the Reading Company appointed David O'Neil, a University of Pennsylvania graduate with little business experience but an upbeat vision of the market's future, to the new job of general manager of the ailing market. Slowly but steadily, the dismal slide ended and, in fact, the market began a dramatic turnaround.

Opposite. An empty stall in 1980 had managed to retain many of its original construction features. This was about the time that the market began its modern renaissance. (David O'Neil Collection; courtesy of the Atwater Kent Museum)

Below. Just before being converted to soup, a monster sea turtle draws an appreciative crowd at a seafood stand in the 1950s. (Frank Weer Collection)

Changes were inevitable. Improvements in the food-distribution system used by supermarkets had wiped out the advantage locally grown produce once held, and that had resulted in a reduction in the number of truck farms in the surrounding rural areas. Other farmers switched to growing scarce specialties that soon made the market an epicure's delight. Those with little time to cook at home sought prepared food with special appeal. That led to the appearance of a dozen small booths featuring ethnic or other non-traditional menu items that could be eaten at lunchtime at nearby tables. Other dedicated patrons were the elderly and low-income Center City residents who learned they could stretch their tight budgets by shopping at the market.

The variety and quality of often-scarce foodstuffs available in the heart of the city was a delightful revelation to the affluent young urban population during O'Neil's 10-year tenure, and the market prospered.

The train shed above, meantime, fell silent in 1985 when the city's commuter-rail system was rerouted to bypass the terminal. After several years of negotiations and false starts, the Pennsylvania Convention Center Authority was created to convert the Reading Terminal into a spectacular entranceway to the new convention center. Philadelphians—with fire in their eyes—immediately demanded assurances that the venerable gustatory jewel under the silent tracks would be part of the terminal's rehabilitation plan.

That would not be simple, since there were pressing engineering requirements to strengthen the foundation of the train shed just where the market was located. That brought up concern, echoing the situation a century before, about how the standholders could tide themselves over through the disruptions of the construction period.

When the Pennsylvania Convention Center Authority took over the project in late 1990, Bill Gardiner, an experienced market manager and onetime assistant to O'Neil, was hired to run the market. As was the case in 1892, the market's 1992 farmers and merchants were able, with some understandable aches and pains, to endure the discomforts of the 18-month transition period and begin to settle into a reborn Reading Terminal Market that has lost little of its traditional charm.

When the refurbishing job was completed, descendants of three of the earliest standholder families agreed it had been done with surprising panache and sensitivity. "They've done a remarkable job," said Harry G. Ochs, whose namesake grandfather founded the Ochs meat business in 1906. "The work really was needed, cleaning the place up, rewiring everything. And they did it without making it too glitzy." Ochs, who is chairman of the Reading Terminal Market Merchants' Association, said he does not expect to sell much meat to the convention crowds. His concern is making sure hordes of conventioneers don't discourage his steady customers—some of them grandchildren of regular patrons of his own grandfather—from continuing to buy their special meats from him.

The Bassett Ice Cream stand bears the oldest name in the market. Louis DuBois Bassett formed his firm in 1861 and was among the charter members of the new market when it was built in 1893. Today ice cream cones and sundaes are dispensed over a venerable marble counter that survived a move of the Bassett stand during the rehabilitation. The manager, Mike Strange, is a Bassett, son of former owner Anne Bassett, and a great-great-grandson of Louis. He enthuses:

The market is 100 percent better than it was. And it still has the old flavor. Of course, we're benefiting from the convention crowds because we have a "quick walkaway" trade.

Another old name at the market is Margerum, whose patriarch, William B. Margerum, conducted a successful butcher business that, until World War II, was the biggest purveyor of meats on the East Coast. Today his great-granddaughter, Noelle Margerum, has converted the family's market stand to specialty foods, from herbs and spices to rare condiments and other comestibles. She has two nephews and a niece who, she assumes, will continue the Margerum name as part of the century-old Terminal Market tradition.

It is a testament to the power of that tradition that many of its older patrons regard the Ochses, Bassetts, and Margerums—along with other Reading Market names like Halteman, Moyer and Spataro—as comfortable and familiar fixtures of the past, a personal link to a Philadelphia treasure house of food.

Left and below. *Four generations of the Ochs family have been prominent stand-holders at the market since 1906. The second Harry G. Ochs is shown in the straw boater at left in his butcher stand with his son, Harry III, in 1947. Below, the younger Harry Ochs, wearing a hat similar to his father's in the other photo, poses with his sons—Nicholas (front) and Harry IV—in the 1990s version of the Ochs meat stand. (Archival photograph courtesy of Harry G. Ochs; hat courtesy of the Atwater Kent Museum; current photograph, Carol M. Highsmith, Photographer)*

There was curiosity, and there were expectations, as electrification's hot wires came to Reading Terminal. Of course some tradition-bound railroaders scowled as they beheld the glistening bronze strands being stretched along a forest of gantries and overhead girders on the viaduct past Race Street tower and into the sanctum of the train shed.

But for most commuters the $20 million project would mean faster schedules and cleaner riding, and for the company, the efficiencies of electrification would translate into a heftier bottom line.

The work began in June 1929 with groundbreaking at Wayne Junction for a new shop, equipped to repair and maintain the Reading's soon-to-be-delivered fleet of 130 multiple-unit coaches, each capable of operating on its own—or in combinations of two or more—without a locomotive. At about the same time, 1,500 workers began erecting the catenary system used to carry the energized wires between the Reading Terminal and Jenkintown.

The four-track viaduct out Ninth Street from the terminal to 16th Street Junction required the most amount of work, with the wires strung on portal-type steel crossbeams supported by H-sections 300 feet apart. Inside the train shed itself, the wires were suspended from the roof by cables that were steadied laterally by another row of cables spanning the width of the shed.

Electrified service began at 3:01 a.m. (the Reading had a penchant for pre-dawn inaugurals) on Sunday, June 26, 1931, when Train No. 532 for West Trenton, New Jersey—Harry J. Grill, assistant road foreman of engines, at the controls—glided out of the terminal with little more than a whisper. Three hours, 15 minutes later, the first incoming electric train, No. 2222 from Hatboro, Pa., rocked quietly into its berth under the arched roof.

Taxis jostle for position, and shoppers jam Market Street in front of Reading Terminal at the height of its service as an all-purpose rail depot just before the renovation of the late 1940s. That change, among other things, obliterated the six graceful arches visible along the front of the company office building. (Reading Company Employees' Magazine)

It would be almost two years before "juice" was extended to Norristown and Chestnut Hill because of the elevated construction necessary. That brought the total electrified route out of the terminal to 84.14 miles. In 1966 electric service was installed on the Fox Chase Line and extended from Hatboro to Warminster eight years later.

The atmosphere around the busy train shed underwent a profound change after electrical propulsion was introduced. There were new noises—the subdued whine of traction motors and the hiss of pantographs sliding under trolley wires—that provided a metallic-sounding backdrop to the staccato crack of exhausts from the diminished stable of steam locomotives.

Visual changes were more subtle, since the pillars of gray smoke and billows of white steam generated by the remaining steam engines continued to pervade the open expanses under the train shed's high roof. But there was somewhat less switching on the maze of 13 tracks, since the electric cars did not have to be serviced and turned between runs as the steam equipment did.

Each weekday in the late 1920s, the train shed saw 160 departures and 157 arrivals, all powered by steam, with an average of 20,000 passengers daily. By the end of World War II, total arrivals and departures had increased slightly—to 350 from 317—but by that time fewer than a third of those movements were powered by steam engines. And the number of passengers, the majority of them commuters, had increased to around 50,000 daily.

Still, steam locomotives dominated activities on the train floor. The terminal was home to two-score big Pacific-class engines assigned to the heavier trains on the Main Line, the Bethlehem Branch, and the New York Division. These were modern locomotives that could hold their own with the best passenger steam engines on short-haul service anywhere in the late steam era.

The rest of the long-distance passenger work was handled by the Reading's large stable of older "camelbacks"—locomotives with the enginemen's cabs nestled over the middle of the boiler instead of over the rear. That unusual configuration was developed by the old Philadelphia & Reading to facilitate burning anthracite in wide fireboxes that left little room for a cab at the back of the engine. The Reading's fast runners that dueled the Pennsylvania Railroad's flyers at the turn of the century all were center-cab engines.

Long-distance travelers received more attention from the terminal staff than did commuters, although the distinction between the two, due to the relatively short main and branch lines (the longest passenger run, to Williamsport, Pa., was just 199 miles), would blur as the suburbs encroached on the Quaker State countryside. Just about every regular intercity train entering the terminal carried its hardy band of daily riders from Pottsville or Reading, Bethlehem or Allentown, along with crowds of day-trippers.

An electric-powered commuter train glides into its berth in the train shed, an occurrence that happened hundreds of times each weekday after the suburban lines were electrified in the early 1930s. (Richard Short, Photographer)

54

Once inside the terminal, the two types of riders behaved sharply differently. Commuters would dash through the station to the exit nearest their destinations and were gone, swallowed for the day in the midtown warrens of the mercantile world. Returning at day's end, some might pause for a cup of cheer in the terminal restaurant, but many would arrive in the train lobby breathless, just in time to catch their homebound trains.

The more unhurried traveler from upstate had more cause to tarry in the terminal, taking advantage of its own little world of comforts and services. On the second floor, beyond the train floor, these included the Roma Brothers' eight-chair barber shop and a bootblack stand alongside the men's room at the east end of the concourse. On the other side was the lunchroom, with its oval counter where the women among the arriving day-trippers could stop for a cup of tea while they finalized plans for their forays into the city. For many of them, a trip downstairs to the Reading Terminal Market would be a mandatory stop.

Next to the plebeian lunchroom was the more formal dining room. During the late 1920s and into the thirties under the ownership of Louis G. Bauerle—George Knoblauch's former headwaiter—it maintained its classy reputation. The terminal restaurant occupied the southwest corner of the head house second floor, and its clientele was not limited to railroad patrons. Until the dining room was replaced in 1939 by a more downscale eatery called the "Gateway," it attracted discerning diners from throughout the Delaware Valley.

Except for the purchase of tickets or checking of baggage, the first floor of the head house had little to interest passengers. There eventually was a roomful of public telephones and, after 1930, a separate waiting room for passengers of Reading Company motor buses that provided supplementary highway service to eastern Pennsylvania towns and to Atlantic City.

In those relatively early years of the internal combustion engine—before the family car had become an institution—most people who lived in the coal regions up the Schuylkill Valley depended upon Reading trains for travel beyond the reach of local trolley-car systems. For them and thousands of others, a trip to Philadelphia would be a great adventure that the family planned, and for which it saved, well in advance. Such a journey became a tradition in the weeks before Christmas especially, when Mom, Pop, and the kids would ride the steam trains to Reading Terminal before touring Philadelphia's legendary department-store toylands.

A bit of glamour attended activity in the terminal after 1937 when the Reading had the Budd Company of Philadelphia build the first steam-powered streamlined train in the East for two daily round trips on its blue-ribbon route to the shores of New York Harbor at Jersey City (or "New York," as the public-relations people preferred to call it).

Rolling stock for the blue-and-silver train consisted of five cars—two coaches, a diner/cafe car, and two observation cars. The latter would be spotted at each end of the train, so that there would be no need to turn the whole train for its quick turnaround at each end of the run. The locomotive, encased in stainless-steel shrouding to match the cars, would be attached to the front observation car for one leg of the trip; then it would be turned around and backed against the other observation car for the return.

Opposite. *Trains entering or leaving the terminal on the four-track viaduct were controlled from Race Street Tower, just outside the train shed. Train Director Frank McGowan is shown using the "train describer" system, which alerted outlying towers that a train was coming. (Historical Society of Pennsylvania)*

Above. *One of hundreds of Reading employees whose skills and care kept trains operating in and out of the terminal was Stephen E. Bright, a machinist at the company shops in Reading. (Historical Society of Pennsylvania)*

When the train went into regular service on December 13, 1937, it still did not have a formal name. So the company sponsored a contest to find one. After considerable publicity, the winning name was selected, and a dedication ceremony was set for the following February 23. It would turn out to be the most gala event the terminal had ever seen—far more noteworthy and festive than the opening of the terminal itself 45 years earlier.

Thousands of onlookers jammed the train-floor lobby close to the platform for Tracks 2 and 3 on that cold Wednesday evening. Dazzling spotlights lit the area, and rows of special police stood guard. Eager reporters, photographers, and newsreel cameramen shivered as they waited in obedient clusters near the bumper block of Track 3 while most of the company's brass crowded around a tiny, fur-clad woman who was gamely trying to swing a heavy champagne bottle in the general direction of Locomotive No. 117's burnished running gear. She was Lily Pons, star of the Metropolitan Opera, films, and radio. And when the bottle finally smashed against the No. 1 driving wheel, she piped in her million-dollar soprano voice:

I christen thee "Crusader."

The flair of that dedication carried over to the daily operation of the train—at least for a while. The Reading's transportation department at first hand-picked the Crusader's train crews, until the union brotherhoods (locals) objected. But even when they were not chosen for their superior skill or appearance, the men assigned to the streamliner seemed to display an added air of pride. Crewmen wore white gloves, and their uniforms had to be well-fitted and immaculate. They used special ticket punches with side covers to prevent the punched-out pieces from falling onto the train's carpeted floors. Vacuum-cleaning equipment was stored in one car and used at the completion of each run. To try to avoid black smoke, Engines 117 and 118 were fed a special diet of 80 percent soft coal and 20 percent barley-sized grains of hard coal.

A few train-shed hands and train crews could not resist poking fun at the affectations that surrounded the Crusader. One crewman, for example, is said to have been suspended for five days after passengers overheard him referring to the train as a "tin can."

While the streamliner helped upgrade the Reading's "Yorker" service, it paled in convenience alongside the Pennsy's direct service into the heart of Manhattan. To nobody's surprise, it was not long before Crusader's two daily round trips were reduced to one. It continued to carry the Reading's banner on the New York Division through World War II, however, and well into the troubled post-war period. Its shining locomotive was finally replaced by a déclassé diesel in 1966.

Above. *A welder at the Budd Company plant in Philadelphia works on one of the Crusader cars while it is being fabricated for the Reading. (Historical Society of Pennsylvania)*

Opposite. *Most of the steam locomotives that hauled trains in and out of the terminal were designed and built at the company shops in Reading. An apprentice is seen here adjusting the valve on a heavy passenger engine in the shops for routine maintenance. (Historical Society of Pennsylvania)*

Some of the men assigned to Reading Terminal duty served their entire careers at 12th and Market. But many more were the products of a different kind of railroading. Several mid-level supervisory jobs at the terminal were given as "promotions" to uplanders, and not always did these men accustomed to the tough grades of the Catawissa Branch, or the busy tracks of the freight yard in the city of Reading, consider the assignment a reward. Those who did move to the terminal brought an informal style that produced an atmosphere different from the stuffy air so prevalent over at the Pennsy's Broad Street Station. The easy camaraderie among the car inspectors, stationmasters, baggage handlers, train callers, and other regulars in the terminal operation could be heard in their conversations—the flat brogue of the Schuylkill "coal crackers" or the Pennsylvania Dutch patois of the Berks County men competing with the locals' distinctive Philadelphia twang.

Names were usually modified to the ultra-diminutive— James becoming "Jimmy" (not Jim); Thomas, "Tommy," and so forth—the adolescent nickname clinging to them even in their 60s or when they became senior officials of the company. More-colorful nicknames appeared, too, reflecting the men's appearances or backgrounds: "Snowshoes," "The Judge," "Hungry Joe," "Donald Duck," "Windy," "Ragweed," "Fire Chief," "Bones," "The Redhead," "Tombstone," "Cinnamon Bun Joe," and "The Flying Dutchman" were just some of them.

The last, whose formal name was Joe Schmeig, kept a quart-sized cream container filled with coffee alongside the hot engine boiler in his camelback cab. His nickname came from his German background (Pennsylvanians making the common mistake of confusing *Deutsch* with "Dutch"). Schmeig was a noted "hard-runner" who could squeeze maximum speed out of his iron steed. His thick Pennsylvania Dutch accent did him little good at the outbreak of World War II when, as a vacationer in Germany, he found himself and his son interned until a hefty bribe could buy them their freedom.

Practical jokes among terminal workers were as inevitable as the seasons. They ranged from applying slippery graphite powder to firemen's shovels to staging phony "turkey raffles," in which the "winner" received a paper bag filled with the carcass of a bird provided by a cooperative Terminal Market merchant.

Then there was the time an engineer on one of the clockers explained his late arrival in the terminal one evening by claiming a pheasant had flown into his headlight a few miles outside town, requiring him to run his darkened engine at slow speed, blowing his whistle and ringing his bell, for the final dozen miles into Philadelphia.

Road Foreman of Engines George Clauser, a no-nonsense "Dutchman" from Reading, asked suspiciously, "Vere ist diss bird?" The battered corpse of a pheasant (source never completely verified) was delivered to Clauser's office, and the engineer was duly absolved of blame for his tardy arrival.

One of Reading Terminal's best-known denizens was Bobby Linden, a gregarious passenger trainman on the York-ers, who as a 17-year-old high school student had ridden the Crusader on its first revenue run in 1937. That experience inspired Linden to become a railroader—and specifically to aspire to a job on the handsome streamliner he had beheld with wonder that day. It took a few years and a detour in military service during World War II before the ebullient Lansdale resident realized his dream.

The Depression had nibbled away at the array of trains operating in and out of the terminal, but passenger traffic was up marginally in the early 1940s until Japan attacked Pearl Harbor. After that, the flood of young servicemen and women jammed the terminal and brought back memories of its halcyon years. A USO canteen—the United Services Organization, a civilian-organized group that supplied off-duty comforts to service personnel—was set up in what had been the ladies' waiting room. A group of company officials' wives volunteered to host GIs who were waiting for trains, and by war's end, more than 250,000 servicemen and women had accepted the USO's hospitality.

A somber reminder of the war was a huge service flag, bearing the number of company employees in the armed forces and an updated total of casualties, hung from a flag-pole on the Market Street face of the head house. By V-J Day, the flag bore the number 81 in its gold star, depicting the number of employees killed from among the 3,959 known to have served in the military.

Early in the war, jittery civilian defense authorities held air-raid drills and ordered Reading Company officials to black out the five skylights in the train-shed roof to prevent light, which might guide enemy aircraft, from shining skyward at night. Unfortunately this also kept sunlight out, casting a gloom over the train shed that became permanent after the war when the glass was removed and replaced with waterproof roofing.

The onset of war had, however, spurred a sentimental Reading Terminal tradition that warmed the spirits of travelers around Christmas and Easter for years. About 75 Reading employees organized the Reading Choral Society for the Christmas season in 1942. It trolled yuletide carols at noon daily in the waiting room. So successful were the performances that the society returned at Eastertime to sing appropriate hymns of that season.

Midway through the war, the terminal passed its 50th birthday with no more formal fuss than had been lavished upon its opening in January 1893.

The war ended with rising hopes of a strong resurgence of intercity passenger travel, and the Reading eagerly made ready for the expected boom. Few realized it, but the postwar period would soon see an end to the all-purpose role for which the old Reading Terminal had been designed more than half a century earlier.

**W**ith the war's economic restrictions and material shortages behind it, the United States in the late 1940s looked forward not just to an era of peace, but also to a new kind of world made infinitely easier and more luxuriant by some of the astounding new technologies that had been developed to win the conflict. The Reading Company, like the entire railroad industry, shared in those heady prospects, especially the forecasts of reinvigorated passenger-train travel.

The façade of the Reading head house takes on a much more commercial look than its original Italianate appearance after the "modernization" of 1948. (Frank Weer Collection)

Accordingly, President R.W. Brown and his managers in 1947 set in motion a comprehensive overhaul and modernization of the Reading's passenger service and facilities, an ambitious program that would continue into the early 1950s.

Although ridership in 1946 had shown a 12½-percent decline from the peak of 25 million passengers in the final year of the war, the Reading—along with the rest of the industry—figured that such a post-war sag was simply the public's temporary readjustment to peacetime. Thus the company confidently went ahead with its plans to upgrade both its trains and its biggest terminal.

The new trains were dazzling compared to the drab pre-war equipment they replaced. The makeover started with the motive power, with construction at Reading shops in 1947 of 10 brand-new steam locomotives (the last such machines built for any Class 1 American railroad), powerful and handsome Pacifics trimmed with graceful gold striping. They would provide high-performance power for three new deluxe passenger trains, as well as the 10-year-old, silver-toned Crusader.

The other trains, sporting two-tone green, semi-streamlined cars, replaced existing express trains—the "Wall Street" joining the Crusader on the New York run, and the "Schuylkill" and "King Coal" operating with unaccustomed verve on Main Line schedules to Pottsville and Shamokin, respectively. Their subsequent comings and goings beneath the huge train-shed roof in Philadelphia provided a new aura of modernity and glamour to the Market Street depot even as the structure was undergoing its own refurbishing.

The terminal's two-year modernization—company flacks liked to call it "streamlining"—cost well over a million dollars and was not completed until 1949. The new look covered or obliterated much of the original Victorian decor of the terminal, and it was generally applauded by a war-weary public that was trying to accommodate "old-fashioned" tastes within a rapidly evolving technological world.

Exterior alterations to the head house were the most controversial, particularly the decision to brick up the six graceful arches above the second-floor loggia along Market Street. Other delicate embellishments on the upper portions of the 1893 Italianate face of the building were similarly modified or removed. Additionally, several new shops adorned with slabs of stainless steel and gaudy neon replaced subdued establishments on the ground floor along Market Street. And the building's majestic black marquee, bearing the company's diamond-shaped logo on each flank and covering the full width of the sidewalk along half the length of the building, was replaced by a stainless-steel canopy of slick design and modest proportions.

There was one improvement that was universally applauded. The soot-covered exterior of the building was sandblasted back to its original pink-and-white patina, in sharp contrast to the rest of the deteriorating neighborhood east of City Hall.

Improvements inside the passenger area, while embracing the streamlined motif, were generally practical rather than cosmetic. New high-speed escalators whisked passengers to the train floor and waiting room from both the Market and 12th Street entrances. A new, modernistic ticket window, looking somewhat like a flying saucer about to soar off to Pottsville, was erected on the north wall of the waiting room; and that once-stately chamber was crunched to half its original impressive height by a false ceiling with modern lighting.

But the most distressing alteration for admirers of the old terminal was the removal of the handsome iron gates from the train concourse, to be replaced by a sterile-looking wall with plain doors leading to the platform. A contemporary newspaper account described it this way: "The old swinging doors between the waiting room and the train concourse have been torn away, and so has the iron picket fence separating the concourse from the tracks." Picket fence, indeed!

Reading train crewmen huddle around a radio on a baggage cart in May of 1946, waiting to learn whether a threatened nationwide railroad strike would be called off. It wasn't, and the three days it lasted were one of the few times service in Reading Terminal was disrupted. (Historical Society of Pennsylvania)

In the midst of these physical alterations, another important change was taking place in the makeup of the terminal's patronage. While the number of riders on short-haul suburban trains had increased to a substantial 50,000 carried on about 300 commuter trips in and out of the terminal each day, the total annual passenger count had been steadily ebbing since the end of the war: just under 20 million in 1947, then down to an alarming 13½ million in 1950. One-third of the traffic strained the terminal's resources in the morning and evening rush-hour dashes each weekday. Inevitably, Reading Terminal was becoming a commuter station, as its long-distance Pullman accommodations and the traditional service for occasional riders from the coal regions and the farm country upriver steadily disappeared from Reading timetables.

In retrospect, the terminal's physical changes, whether by accident or design, can be seen to have anticipated just such a fundamental transformation. Despite the glitz and state-of-the-art hardware installed in 1948, few of the new appointments served the comfort of tarrying passengers. Reading Terminal had been made over into a busy metropolitan foyer, designed for the rapid movement of masses of people whose daily presence would be brief and undistracted.

To management's chagrin, in the first year after the new equipment and improvements at the terminal were put in service the number of passengers riding all the Reading's various trains continued its postwar plunge, this time by a devastating 19 percent. Inexplicably to the company, the public—which loved to watch the proud new locomotives and handsome coaches racing past at speed—was losing interest in paying to *ride* in them.

What had happened to that promise of America's eager return to train travel? The *private automobile*—and government-subsidized highways for them to run on—were what had happened. In the area served by the Reading, the eastern extension of the Pennsylvania Turnpike was completed in 1950, making auto travel from the middle Schuylkill Valley to Philadelphia comfortable, fast, and economical. Shortly afterward, the New Jersey Turnpike slithered alongside the Reading's New York Division tracks like a deadly serpent, threatening the company's refurbished Yorkers to Jersey City more effectively than the Pennsy's tuscan-colored clockers ever could.

By 1950 the company realized the great passenger-train revival was not to be, and a period of slow and quiet retrenchment of service beyond the suburbs began. Within five years after they were built, the 10 handsome new steam engines were removed from duty on the new trains, and in another five years they were cut apart with torches and sold for scrap. While they were being shunted off to their destruction, only a handful of their older steam cousins remained intact anywhere on the system.

On May 6, 1952, an older version of the Reading Pacific class, No. 134, had the dubious honor of being the last steam engine to haul a revenue run into the terminal when the 28-year-old engine substituted for a crippled diesel on a commuter train from Newtown. Four months later No. 134, too, was at a salvage yard, swept up in the campaign to do away with every steam passenger engine on company property.

The internal-combustion engine had been showing up in the train shed in various diesel configurations throughout the post-war period. The big black, green, and gold F-T 7s that fronted the company's streamliners on the New York Division and the Main Line quickly began to win over admirers as they growled in and out of their assigned tracks beginning in 1950. But old-timers complained about the "offensive smell" of the fuel-oil exhaust.

A new breed of sport-shirted technicians, skilled in the use of electronics and modern communications, had suddenly joined the terminal's denim-clad work force of car and air-brake inspectors, and steam-locomotive mechanics. The initial relationship was an uneasy one. But, as it had with the advent of the electric cars, the post-steam world of the new Reading Terminal soon settled down to reliable railroading.

Baggage man Walter Pollick checks grips in the terminal's baggage room, where he had worked for more than half of his 72 years when the photograph was taken in 1946. (Historical Society of Pennsylvania)

There was irony for the Reading in other events of the early 1950s. Even as the terminal was getting used to its new role as a glorified bus station, its onetime nemesis, the Pennsy's venerable Broad Street Station, ceased operations in 1952. The Pennsylvania's commuter functions moved underground to its Suburban Station, and its long-distance service moved to the 30th Street Station to the west. The Gothic Broad Street Station, its train shed, and its viaduct carrying tracks from the west were razed the following year to make room for high-rise office buildings.

There was little reason for the Reading to gloat at this turn of events. For one thing, the removal of the Broad Street Station and its cumbersome viaduct prompted some municipal voices—in the name of then-fashionable "urban renewal"—to demand that the Reading Terminal and the Ninth Street viaduct meet the same fate. And the Reading had its own troubles with its ever-worsening passenger-revenue deficits.

A succession of marketing projects, supported by government funding, provided some help to keep the costs of commuter operations from dragging down the entire corporation. "Operation Northwest," featuring low fares on the Chestnut Hill Branch, was the first effort, beginning in October 1958. A similar project on the Fox Chase line, dubbed "Operation Northeast," went into effect the next year, to be followed by "Operation Shawmont" on the Norristown Branch.

Below. Brand new diesel engine 473 prepares to head out of the terminal with a train in May 1952 about the time the last steam engine worked a regular passenger trip into the train shed. (Robert J. Linden, Photographer)

Overleaf. Massive crowds filled the terminal's train concourse as Philadelphia's streetcar and bus drivers went on strike in January 1953. The railroad put on extra trains to handle the additional passengers and won glowing tributes from city officials and newspapers afterward for its performance. (Urban Archives, Temple University, Philadelphia)

The Reading Company demonstrated its alarm by organizing a task force in 1958, headed by Vice President Paul Gangewere, to do a thorough study of the commuter situation and come up with future options. This move was prompted in part by a city planning agency recommendation that the Reading and Pennsylvania commuter lines be joined underground somewhere around the Reading Terminal, to allow run-through operations from the northern suburbs served by the Reading to the towns to the south and west that were the Pennsy's commuter domain. Although the Reading's president, Joseph A. Fisher, and his Pennsy counterpart, James Symes, met to discuss the idea, the scheme received little support from politicians and the press when it was revealed, and it would languish for years with only occasional public attention.

The 1960s saw a succession of new disasters for Reading Terminal and its operations. The first was on November 16, 1960, when a million-dollar fire wrecked the terminal's old powerhouse just outside the train shed at Cherry Street. The blaze shut down all train service into the terminal, but a disaster plan enabled passengers to bypass the fire scene on buses that shuttled between the terminal and the North Broad Street Station, three miles away.

A similar problem arose three years later when fire destroyed a factory building along the Ninth Street viaduct beyond North Broad Street. The blaze destroyed the railroad's tower controlling traffic at Diamond Street, shutting down service on the viaduct. This time the company used a batch of newly acquired rail diesel cars out of the terminal along the Pennsylvania Avenue Subway to the Schuylkill River on the same route used by Main Line trains in the first years of the terminal's operation.

A week later another emergency, caused by a strike of city transit employees, put the terminal and its staff to another test, this one lasting 19 days. An estimated half-million extra riders swarmed in and out of the terminal during that crisis.

But other non-operating difficulties had piled up swiftly during those years. As 1962 began, Gangewere, who had just succeeded Fisher as president, announced the company had lost $6.25 million the previous year. It was the Reading's first deficit of the century. A year later, the U.S. Post Office Department and the Railway Express Company advised railroads they would be withdrawing their mail and package business from intercity trains in favor of trucks. That represented a $2.5 million revenue loss to the Reading, but it allowed the railroad to drop a number of long-distance trains that had continued to operate almost exclusively to carry mail and packages.

By this time federal, state, and local governments had become aroused about the deteriorating commuter situation on both the Reading and the Pennsylvania suburban lines. Three agencies came into existence in the late 1950s and early sixties to support the carriers.

Above. *Newspaper ads showed off the comfort and cleanliness of the new equipment that the Reading introduced to most of its long-haul trains out of the terminal in the late 1940s. Neither ads nor the improved appointments did much good, as train ridership continued to decline. (Reading Company Employees' Magazine)*

Opposite. *A trackman glumly surveys the scene after service inside the terminal was shut down by a fire in the depot's old power plant in November 1960. An emergency plan, using shuttle buses from the terminal to the North Broad Street Station, provided a semblance of effective service until the damage was repaired. (Urban Archives, Temple University, Philadelphia)*

74

The nonprofit Passenger Service Improvement Corporation (PSIC) was formed by the city of Philadelphia to help fund special ridership programs such as Operation Northwest and Operation Northeast. PSIC also bought 12 new rail diesel cars and 17 sleek "Silverliner" cars that were then leased to the Reading.

The Southeastern Pennsylvania Transportation Compact (SEPACT), involving the city and three adjoining counties, was intended to provide financial help to operations outside the city, ensuring service—at least for a while—beyond the suburban area as far as Pottsville and Bethlehem.

Finally, and most important to the Reading, was the Southeastern Pennsylvania Transportation Authority (SEPTA), which was formed in 1964 under state auspices to eventually take over operation of the region's ailing bus, streetcar, and commuter-rail systems.

In 1965 the Reading and SEPTA launched "Operation Reading," under which the transit authority came close to the administrative takeover of the railroad's commuter service. One of the first actions by the new partnership was the refurbishing of 38 of the Reading's original multi-unit electric cars from their olive-drab to an attractive blue-and-cream color scheme, earning them their new nickname: the "blue geese." Most of these cars would soldier on in service until 1991, when they were auctioned of to various museums and rail-fan groups.

Within a few years only a handful of Reading trains served passengers on a Main Line schedule that terminated in Pottsville, with service on the Bethlehem Branch similarly reduced. Jersey City service was only a shadow of what it had been just a decade earlier, with diesel cars—one train still called the Crusader—doing all the work. In fact, there was only one regularly scheduled conventional train with locomotives (one diesel unit at each end) operating on the entire railroad: a daily push-pull round-trip from Reading.

Virtually every facet of the railroad's operations by this time was losing money. Annual losses for passenger service alone averaged $6 million. Hauling coal and merchandise managed to make a modest profit that was easily offset by the growing cost of hauling people.

As the Reading waged its losing battle to stay solvent in the 1960s, there simply was no money available for any expenditure that did not directly support operations. Consequently the aging Reading Terminal, always in need of costly repairs and maintenance, began to tatter. It was a situation that would have been unimaginable in the proud early years.

Passengers grumbled about the decrepit condition of the coaches, which were chronically overcrowded because they were in such short supply. With only 153 spottily maintained cars on the active roster (and a high percentage unserviceable at any one time), the railroad was barely able to meet its basic traffic commitments.

Reading trainman Bobby Linden photographs himself in a mirror decorating the end of a coach on a New York Division "clocker." (Robert J. Linden, Photographer)

Light snow creates a halo-like aura around a Reading electric train as it leaves the terminal, bound for one of Philadelphia's suburbs. (Richard Short, Photographer)

Reading management, headed after 1964 by Charles E. Bertrand, tried desperately to hold off disaster, cutting both its work force and services where possible. Passenger stations beyond the Philadelphia commuter territory were declared surplus and sold whenever a buyer could be found. Included among them was the hulking, derelict white elephant known as the North Broad Street Station.

Nothing was considered off-limits for potential fundraising, not even the Reading Terminal itself. In 1968 the company's real estate department began exploring with developers the idea of converting the 12th and Market property into a multi-purpose commercial complex of stores, a hotel, a bus depot, and a parking garage as part of the new Market Street East plan being pushed by city planners. The Reading Company would be a partner in the project with a development firm.

Under that proposal, the Reading head house would be replaced by a high-rise office building, and the train shed would be spared to provide a lofty cover over a sub-basement bus station and parking area under the market, and a public arboretum above it. The shed would not be needed for rail traffic, since the planners by then were confident a proposed Center City commuter tunnel would soon be a reality. The high-rise idea was bandied about for a time but was soon pushed aside by other worries.

Running the Reading in those days was like organizing a giant yard sale for railroads. Unused day coaches were peddled to other railroads as far away as South America. Even old lanterns, station signs, locomotive number plates, and anything else that a railroad buff might pay a few dollars for were sold off to raise cash. Finally, on November 23, 1971, completely out of cash and bereft of ready credit, the Reading Company threw in the towel, declaring bankruptcy for the fourth time in its history.

For the next five years, as its parent corporation tried to extricate itself from the bonds of receivership, and the city planners struggled to rebuild the neighborhood near 12th and Market into a grand new design, the sprawling Reading Terminal complex did little more than survive. It had become just a shabby shadow of its onetime grandeur as one of the East's great railroad hubs.

It was clear from the beginning of this latest bankruptcy that the company would not survive as a railroad. Economic realities, including outright government subsidies of air travel—would not permit it. There were six other northeast railroads, including the former Pennsylvania (by then a part of the merged Penn Central), mired in bankruptcy as well, and the federal government proposed to put them all together in a system to be called Consolidated Rail Corporation. Except for limited commuter-rail service, Conrail was primarily a freight operation. Long-distance passenger-rail travel had been turned over to the quasi-government Amtrak system, whose relatively high-speed "Metroliner" service between Washington and New York—stopping in Philadelphia—was a hit, reviving interest in train travel through the Northeast Corridor.

In the course of the negotiations that finally led to the Conrail solution, the fate of the Reading Terminal—including the terminal market—was considered mainly in terms of its sale or salvage value.

With diminishing resources and under a blanket of uncertainty, the operating staff at 12th and Market streets kept the trains moving in and out of the terminal as best they could in those painful months of 1975. SEPTA tried to help, but only added to Bertrand's problems by continually falling behind on its support payments to the impoverished railroad.

Finally, all the planning was completed, negotiations ended, and a date was set in the spring of the Bicentennial Year of 1976 for the start-up of the new Conrail system. With it would come the demise of the 143-year-old Reading Railroad.

The date set was April 1, 1976: April Fool's Day.

Opposite. In its final years under Reading Company management, the terminal's daily roster of motive power was mostly electric, multiple-unit trains of various vintage and decor, as is seen in this view across the bumper blocks and train concourse. (Howard Pincus, Photographer)

Above. One lonely passenger with luggage—a rarity at the Reading Terminal by 1974 when this shot was taken— waits forlornly to board his train just before the start of an afternoon rush hour. (Urban Archives, Temple University, Philadelphia)

REBIRTH

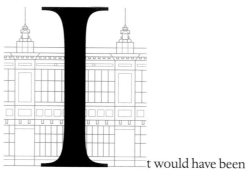

I t would have been difficult to conjure up any warm feelings about the Reading Terminal in those post-Reading years beyond old-timers' wistful sense of nostalgia. Younger commuters, picking their way through the raggedy innards of the once-proud depot, could only wish for something cleaner and more cheerful.

In the midst of the debasement that time and circumstances had forced upon the old terminal by the spring of 1976, there were two related questions about its future: Would a long-discussed Center City commuter-rail tunnel become a reality? And if it did, what would be the fate of the big railroad station under which the tunnel would burrow?

The Reading Company's managers and bankruptcy trustees had been floating a variety of schemes for conversion of their valuable Market Street property once the company got out of the railroad business. All were tied to the city's ambitious Market Street East plan, in which the terminal complex would be the western anchor for a pair of underground shopping malls called Gallery I and Gallery II.

Unexpectedly, the key question about the terminal's future was answered in 1975, when Frank Rizzo—a former police chief who served two lively terms as Philadelphia mayor—parlayed a friendship with former President Richard Nixon into approval of a bill, signed by President Gerald Ford, authorizing federal funding for most of the cost of the Philadelphia commuter-rail project. Within two years, work began on the once widely maligned project that would cost $330 million by the time it was finished six years later. It would connect the Reading and Pennsylvania suburban lines in Center City, providing a more convenient and efficient regional commuter-rail system.

With all of its other troubles, the Reading Terminal's head house and train shed had become architectural lame ducks—their futures acutely in question and their upkeep a day-to-day struggle.

The terminal's owner, the bankrupt non-rail remnants of the Reading Company, had no money to spend on fixing up the sprawling albatross; its operator, Conrail, wanted out of the money-gobbling passenger business, and SEPTA, which leased the depot on behalf of Conrail, could never seem to make its subsidy payments on time, let alone keep the terminal in proper repair.

Nobody at the Reading had much to say, publicly, about the future of the Reading Market because of the uncertainty about the terminal above it.

The Reading Company, which emerged from bankruptcy in 1980, launched a determined search for a way to cash in on its terminal's excellent downtown location. In the words of Bill Dimeling, the company's executive vice president at the time, the idea of turning it into some kind of convention center "simply evolved." He recalled walking along Market Street toward the terminal one day in the early 1980s with a Philadelphia business leader when the subject of Philadelphia's dearth of modern facilities to compete with other eastern cities for the lucrative convention business came up. "We were looking right at the answer," said Dimeling. "That monster train shed with its roof looming over the neighborhood like a colossal dirigible hangar suggested that such a role might be just the thing for it."

In the meantime, officials in the new city administration of Mayor William J. Green, Jr., were cautiously suggesting that the city might better compete for tourist dollars—might help strengthen Philadelphia as a "destination city"—if it had a modern convention hall, and somebody mentioned the Reading Terminal, among other downtown sites, as a possibility.

After a feasibility study and a request for proposals, which were eventually reduced to three, an elaborate plan prepared by a team of architects hired by the Reading Company was selected in September 1983. It called for the former railroad company to construct a new building housing meeting rooms and a new hall, to be built in a four-square-block area north of the terminal—with the train shed serving as a grand entranceway to the hall—and including a convention hotel to be erected at 12th and Market. All parts of this plan, save for its relatively modest cost estimate, would later fall perfectly in place under other auspices.

While concentrating on its convention-center proposal, the Reading also had undertaken a $200,000 overhaul of the Reading Terminal Market. And in a deal with the city for public access to the new commuter-rail tunnel via the terminal's ground floor, the company restored the façade of the first two floors of the head house along Market Street to its original appearance, including the uncovering of the Florentine arches on the second-floor loggia that had been obscured in 1948.

A few months later, SEPTA demonstrated its strapped financial situation by eliminating all train service into the terminal from beyond the five-county suburban Philadelphia area. That meant the end to passenger operations to the city of Reading on what was the original Philadelphia & Reading main line. And in 1982 Conrail helped push through a new federal law allowing the primarily freight railroad to get out of the passenger business. It promptly turned the Philadelphia commuter service over to SEPTA, the local public-transit authority, which suddenly found itself running a railroad.

With the completion of the tunnel the following year, the bittersweet moment finally arrived that old Reading railroaders and admirers of the terminal had been dreading. The tired old architectural Lady of Market Street, which had carried on the trade of her railroading consort alone for eight years, seven months, and six days after his passing, was herself retired from the railroad business. It had been a melancholy, painful widowhood.

Unlike the occasion of the *first* train to enter the train shed on January 30, 1893, the *last* one was sent off with suitable ceremony and sentimentality on Tuesday night, November 6, 1984. It was a nine-car special made up of some of the original Bethlehem electric cars from 1931 and sponsored by the Philadelphia chapter of the National Railway Historical Society. Aboard, bound for Lansdale, were 600 solemn admirers of the late Reading and its once-magnificent flagship depot.

Before engineer Hughie Jenkins got the final high-ball at precisely 8 o'clock for Extra 9129 North's historic journey, there was a simple ceremony on the nearly deserted concourse in front of Gate 6, with appropriate remarks from officials of the non-railroading Reading Company, SEPTA, and the railroading society.

Minutes after the special swung past Brown Street north of the terminal, SEPTA crews cut off power to the catenary system reaching back to the train shed, and immediately began tearing up the four-track railroad along the old stone viaduct.

A little over a mile away, the Reading Terminal's career as a great railway station had passed into history.

Above. *The glass-enclosed north end of the train shed looms over the floor where wire mesh frames are stacked, ready for laying of the floor. (Carol M. Highsmith, Photographer)*

Opposite. *The distinctive dormer above the exhibition hall concourse gets finishing touches as workmen install the spandrel beam cover. (Carol M. Highsmith, Photographer)*

The convention-center project, after some illusory progress in 1983, quickly bogged down, a victim of Pennsylvania's traditional urban-versus-rural factionalism, which had been compounded by new economic and social strains being felt in all metropolitan areas. The battles revolved around minority participation, sources of funding, and—most important of all—control. Amazingly, these issues were resolved in agreements that became national models for such big civic projects.

One thing was clear from the start: Public funding would be needed, and that would mean some version of public management. The Reading Company agreed to sell the train shed, as well as the old railroad viaduct and other real estate that it owned, to the city, and then withdraw from the project. Only the price remained to be negotiated—a formidable hurdle, as it turned out.

In January 1986 all parties agreed on the creation of a governing body to be known as the Pennsylvania Convention Center Authority (PCCA), which would, as its name implied, *not* be controlled solely by its host city, although it would include some Philadelphia members.

Under a new chairman, Willard G. Rouse III, a prominent Philadelphia downtown developer, the PCCA went ahead with two significant steps. It signed a contract with the Atlanta architectural firm of Thompson, Ventulett, Stainback & Associates—working with the Vitetta Group, Kelly-Maiello, Saxon-Capers and Livingston-Rosenwinkel, all of Philadelphia—to design the new exhibit building and refurbish the train shed. And in October 1987 PCCA began actual demolition of some old buildings north of the shed.

The project became a reality only after its adherents weathered a series of near-catastrophic political battles. The most serious occurred in the spring of 1985, when the Pennsylvania Legislature just barely approved $141 million in funding for the center after defeating the bill in two prior votes. By that time the estimated overall cost of the project was $455 million.

Amid these distractions, not much attention was paid to a 1985 Environmental Protection Agency complaint about hazardous waste in the form of polychlorinated biphenyls on the tracks of the train shed. Such PCBs are used to cool electric motors and are suspected carcinogens. The Reading Company promised to so something about it.

Negotiations for the purchase of the 7½-acre terminal property (excluding the head house) were lengthy and complicated. The $32.2 million sale was finally approved on May 6, 1988 by the City Council, but only after Mayor W. Wilson Goode and Reading officials convinced the council majority to include Reading Terminal Market, pushing the project's overall cost to $523 million. With that assurance, Goode announced triumphantly, "It's now full speed ahead!"

Well, not quite. The deal would not be finalized for two-and-one-half more years, largely because of the PCB cleanup and a series of disagreements between the city and the company over the way it was being handled. Despite that roadblock, official groundbreaking took place on April 17, 1990, with Governor Robert P. Casey, Mayor Goode, and PCCA Chairman Rouse officiating. They announced that the center would be opened for business in May 1993.

The PCB cleanup was finally finished to everyone's satisfaction in November, 1990, and in relatively quick order after the purchase of the train shed and the viaduct was approved, demolition of the latter was begun, and construction of the exhibit hall got underway.

But there would be one more shock. In December, 1991, bids for the work on the reconstruction of the train shed and the market beneath it came in far higher than the PCCA had anticipated. After considerable study and soul-searching, the specifications were scaled back to meet the authority's budgetary limits. After new bids were presented, the overall construction job was awarded to Dick Enterprises of Pittsburgh, which also was building the exhibition hall.

At this point, it had become clear that the restoration work on the train shed—if it were to be done with proper concern for its historic integrity—could not be completed at the same time as the four-square-block convention center behind it. In effect, the project was split in two, with a June 1993 target date set for the huge exhibition hall, and the delicate task of constructing a Grand Hall and great ballroom inside the train shed to be done as soon thereafter as engineering and architectural requirements would allow.

While work proceeded on the exhibition hall north of Arch Street, the train shed — relatively somnolent for six years—came alive with the din of expanded demolition and the start of reconstruction throughout its sprawling interior.

To make up for lost time, the job went ahead on three fronts simultaneously. Before tackling the roof and the old train floor under it, the engineers had to bolster the structural foundations of the shed, and that meant providing new support rods and concrete reinforcements for the huge vertical columns that penetrated far into the foundation below the market. Those members would have to support about 2,000 tons of new steel designed to be part of the refurbished shed.

Up on the old train floor, all the remains of the eight platforms had to be removed before a concrete floor could be laid on the southernmost part of the area. Once that was completed, construction at the north end of a two-story building-within-a-building housing a huge ballroom with meeting rooms underneath it got going.

Above. A crew of surveyors ply their trade inside the train shed. (Carol M. Highsmith, Photographer)

Opposite. The north end of the train shed is visible as the framework for the ballroom is just beginning to rise. Rainwater on the floor reflects the arched open end of the roof. (Carol M. Highsmith, Photographer)

Overleaf. The naked cast-iron skeleton reveals the statue of William Penn atop City Hall three blocks away as workers check out each piece of the century-old train concourse. (Carol M. Highsmith, Photographer)

At the same time, structural crews were refurbishing the 12 pairs of iron trusses that give the roof its graceful shape. A key part of this task was replacing the old iron plates under the cast-iron rollers at the base of the trusses along the west side of the building. The rollers allow the massive roof to move under the weight of snow or in a high wind. In order to lift the roof, a special jack had to be obtained while the new rollers and the iron plates—coated with Teflon—on which they sat were replaced.

Overhead, the temporary roof had to be stripped off, and the purlins—wooden support beams running horizontally between the trusses—checked, and when found to be deteriorated, replaced. To the engineers' dismay, almost 80 percent of the supports were too rotted to use again. Each new purlin had to be specially fashioned from a full pine tree.

In May 1992, as work was beginning on the train shed, newly elected Mayor Ed Rendell announced that the convention center would be run by a combination of public employees and private firms, which helped mute grumbling about who would get the promised jobs that the center would be generating. On October 15, 1991, the last piece of structural steel was set in place in the roof of the main exhibit hall, and the traditional topping-off ceremony took place.

There was one more administrative matter to be taken care of. Harry Perks, who had been boss of the convention-center project for three grueling years of construction and startup, retired in July 1993, and Philadelphia attorney Robert J. Butera became executive director.

With work on the old train shed about half done, the project's handsome new main convention hall was completed in June 1993 and dedicated on the 26th of that month as a kickoff to an 11-day "Welcome America" extravaganza sponsored by the city.

Vice President Al Gore, Lieutenant Governor Mark Singel (representing Governor Casey, who was recovering from surgery), Mayor Rendell and City Council President John Street—with former Mayor Goode and former Governor Dick Thornburgh looking on—took part in a gala ribbon-cutting ceremony at the main entrance. Eight days later South African President F. W. de Klerk and African National Congress Party President Nelson Mandela were feted at a lunch in the hall prior to the presentation to them of the city's Liberty Medal by President Bill Clinton.

In decidedly *un*-Philadelphia style, the project was actually finished on time (minus the train shed for the time being), and within budget ($522 million), and amazed Philadelphians—including many government and business VIPs who gathered for the dedication—were astounded by this upbeat indicator. Rank-and-file citizens turned out for a two-day open house and other events surrounding the festivities in numbers four or five times what had been expected.

What they beheld was a limestone, glass and granite behemoth, sprawling over an area big enough for seven football fields. The two main halls cover 440,000 square feet and include smaller meeting rooms, a 600-seat lecture hall, a huge kitchen with facilities for preparing 10,000 meals a day, and long, spacious external concourses with generous window space facing the busy streets of Center City. Throughout the huge complex are subtle reminders of the old Reading Terminal—the arch motif in the Convention Center's official logo; and many representations of the Industrial Age in the railings, stairways and balconies. The building is topped by seven parallel, curved roofs that echo the great arched roof on the train shed to the south. The center is also graced with $2 million worth of commissioned modern art, distributed throughout the public spaces.

Critics were as positive in their reactions as were ordinary citizens. They praised the architectural team for shoehorning—with grace and imagination—so vast a meeting complex into a crowded downtown area. One wrote that the building, if it were entering an architectural beauty contest, would at a minimum win the "Miss Congeniality" prize; another, perhaps prompted by the remarks of fiction's Kitty Foyle about the old Reading Terminal—"so well behaved"—cited the Convention Center's aesthetic "good manners."

Amid all the hoopla, the north end of the architectural gem that would be the center's ultimate showpiece towered in silence. There was still much work to be done before the restored and transformed train shed could be opened with proper ceremony to complete Philadelphia's unique convention-hall complex.

The imaginative decor can be seen in this view of a corridor in the main exhibit hall. The architecturally striking Pennsylvania Convention Center is filled with original artwork. (Carol M. Highsmith, Photographer)

Opposite. *Vice President*
Al Gore speaks at dedication
ceremonies outside the main
entrance to the new exhibit hall
on June 26, 1993. (Carol M.
Highsmith, Photographer)

One pesky problem was solved in one of those surprising turns that always seemed to characterize the tortuous path of the convention-center project. The problem concerned the head house, the deteriorating Reading office building on Market Street that was supposed to provide an ornate entrance to the train shed. Its fate had been in limbo for five years—with the Reading Company unwilling to reduce its asking price to a level that the city could afford. And nobody else seemed interested in the historic structure.

In a kind of cloak-and-dagger operation just after the dedication of the exhibit hall, the Philadelphia Industrial Development Corporation, using a local realty firm as its agent, outmaneuvered the Reading Company and bought the building for $4.3 million, slightly more than half what the company had been asking. That would enable the architects and engineers to create the kind of grand foyer on Market Street that the regal Grand Hall upstairs deserves. In particular, a new set of escalators from street level to the old train floor level could be installed inside the Market Street entrance to provide a dramatic entry—the "wow! factor," in Rouse's words.

Architect Hyman Myers, vice president of the Vitetta Group that designed the historic portions of the restoration, was asked what visitors looking north from the Market Street end of the concourse would see that would remind them of the terminal's railroading past. Myers, who is a railroad history purist, offered a quick answer:

The first glance into the old train shed will be dominated by the sight of the great roof, with its structural iron supports, especially the trusses curving down from the ridge at the top of the arch to the floor. Then the wall panels, and the restored windows as they looked in 1893 will get their attention. It all has the feel of a train depot.

At the junction of the head house and the short structure linking it to the train shed will be an eight-foot-high steel fence with two gates, representing the original ornamental iron train gates. Just beyond the fence is a row of 12 pylons marking roughly where the bumper blocks were located at the ends of the tracks. And then, embedded in the terrazzo flooring, are 10 pairs of stainless-steel strips running from the pylons toward Arch Street, simulating the tracks.

Sentimentalists among the visitors will visualize something else: the ghosts of millions of travelers and thousands of railroaders of five generations who passed under that great arched roof during its 100 years as a beloved Philadelphia landmark.

Above. *On July 4, 1993, South*
African President F. W. de Klerk
and African National Congress
Party President Nelson Mandela
enter the new convention center
prior to their acceptance of
the Liberty Medal. (Carol M.
Highsmith, Photographer)

Endleaf. *The old train shed—*
now the convention center's
Grand Hall—is still
surmounted by the soaring,
arched backbone of steel. (Carol
M. Highsmith, Photographer)

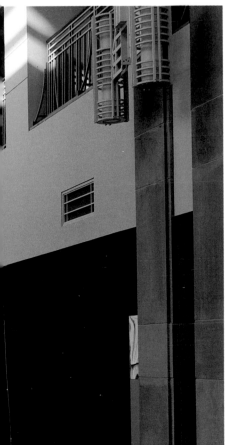